The Unloved Queen

Suniti and her grandmother were shelling peas in the sun.

"Why was I called 'Suniti'?" she asked her grandmother suddenly. "Did you choose the name?"

"I did suggest it," her grandmother admitted. "Everybody thought it was a sweet sounding name."

"Just sweet sounding or does it mean something?" Suniti persisted. She knew that people had the names of gods and goddesses, but she was fairly sure no goddess had ever been called Suniti.

"It means someone who knows how to conduct herself," her grandmother explained. "Someone who knows how to behave properly."

Suniti wasn't sure she always was well behaved. She stole a glance at her grandmother and found her grandmother was smiling at her.

"Are people named according to who they are?" she asked. She knew that the question didn't make sense. But how could she ask whether having a name which meant well behaved made her well behaved?

"Being given a name which means something good is like being given a blessing," her grandmother said. "And yes, you usually are well behaved. And if you aren't sometimes, well, so what? Nobody's perfect!"

Suniti felt better, but she was still thinking about her name. "I suppose," she went on hesitantly, "there's no chance that Suniti was a goddess or at least somebody noteworthy? Who was she?"

It was her grandmother's turn to hesitate. "She was a queen," her grandmother replied.

Suniti brightened. "Was she a great queen?" she asked eagerly. "A much loved queen?"

"Well, no," her grandmother admitted. "She was the unloved queen of a king called Uttanapada, and her son, Dhruva, was his unloved son."

"Why were they unloved?" demanded Suniti.

"I don't know," answered her grandmother.

"What happened to them? What's their story?" Suniti was beginning to feel quite indignant.

"When Dhruva was pushed off his father's lap, he was so hurt he went off to the forest and meditated hard. Well, you know what happens in stories when someone meditates hard," her grandmother said.

"What?" asked Suniti.

"A god appears," her grandmother told her. "And so Lord Vishnu duly appeared and asked Dhruva what he wanted."

"I know what he wanted!" Suniti interrupted.

"What?" asked her grandmother.

"He wanted to be loved," Suniti replied.

"Well, not exactly," her grandmother said. "What he asked for was to be placed so high that he would never again be pushed aside! And that is why, my dear, Dhruva was turned into the Pole Star."

Suniti nodded and took that in. After a pause she asked, "And what about Suniti? What happened to her? Didn't she mind about any of this?"

For a moment Suniti's grandmother didn't know what to say. Then she said, "Well, no. She was well behaved, you see. Still, in some versions of the story, she also became a star, though not a fixed star like Dhruva."

Suniti looked at her grandmother. "It says in my physics book that because of the continuous drift of the stars in relation to the earth's axis, pole stars change over the years."

"I see," said her grandmother. "And what else does your physics book say?"

"It says," Suniti told her, "that every star is a mighty sun!"

Her grandmother laughed. "And which do you like better? Physics or myth?"

"It depends on what they're telling me!" Suniti replied as she tipped the last of the peas into the bowl and watched them bounce among the other peas.

Blue

*I*t so happened that Suniti fell in love with blue.

"Why blue?" her friend protested. "The universe is wide. Why confine yourself to the colour blue?"

"Have you ever cracked your head against the sky? Blue is boundless," she informed her friend.

And seeing that her friend was suitably subdued, she went on to explain that Lawrence of Arabia had owed his success almost entirely to the colour of his eyes. "They thought they could see the sky through his head. And that disarmed them."

Her friend looked doubtful, but Suniti was unstoppable.

"And then there's the Bower Bird, that most courtly of creatures. He decks his bower with fragments of blue, shards of blue glass, iridescent feathers, petals of blue flowers and even scraps of blue paper. And she, with her discerning eye, attuned to precise and varying blueness, chooses entirely by the balance of blue."

"But that's only one colour!" her friend interrupted.

Suniti ignored this. "The pale blue of a robin's eggs has been noted, and the deep, dark green, which is almost blue, of an emu's eggs should also be noted."

"They say," she continued, "that the thirteenth moon in a calendar year is a blue moon. In my opinion they are mistaken. A true blue moon is the moon's outline filled by the smooth and tangible blue of the night sky.

"Blue is Mary's colour, and blue gleams off the skin of Hindu gods. And furthermore, why the sea is blue is also known as The Raman Effect."

Suniti paused and her friend rushed in, "Please. I myself like a variety of colours. Does that mean we can't be friends?"

"Oh no," Suniti smiled a beatific smile. "Blue is bountiful. Quarrels with no one. Clashes with nothing. Blue is the colour of what one loves best. Blue darkens into midnight, and fades into daylight. Lovers of blue," Suniti concluded triumphantly, "efface themselves!"

Kingfisher

A kingfisher who lived on the Axe estuary had practised so hard and become so proficient that in the end she had become a celebrity. Young kingfishers came from far and near to ask for tips.

"Is it," asked one earnest thing, "a matter of understanding the theory perfectly? Should one be able to calculate the angle of refraction, the veering vectors of one or more fish and the precise path of one's own trajectory, before one proceeds to the practice of fishing?"

The kingfisher sighed. She hadn't understood what he was talking about. Probably about fishing. That was all anybody ever talked about. After a pause she murmured slowly, "It all depends, don't you see?"

"On what?" cried the young one. At last they were getting to the heart of it.

"On the angle of the wind," said the kingfisher firmly.

"Thank you! Oh thank you!" came the reply. He spent the rest of his life building wind socks to calibrate the speed and direction of the wind.

Another kingfisher had her own ideas about the nature of fishing.

"Madame Kingfisher," she bubbled enthusiastically, "I am, as you must have guessed, a fan of yours. But be honest. Just between us, it's all a matter of luck, isn't it?"

"I have been fortunate," admitted the kingfisher.

"Well, if I fished on the Axe estuary, and sat on the precise spot where you are sitting, in brief, if I were you, I too would catch a great many fish, would I not?" demanded the fan.

"Undoubtedly," the kingfisher answered, and the fan flew away to tell the world how right she had been.

And so they came and went, until at last, when the kingfisher was old, a very tiny kingfisher arrived.

"I've retired," muttered the old kingfisher.

"It doesn't matter," replied the little one. "I want to learn whatever it is you want to teach."

"All right," grunted the kingfisher. "Sit down and wait."

The little kingfisher sat down and waited. "Right," she said. "Now what?"

"Think."

The little kingfisher thought. After a while she said, "I've thought and I've waited. I've waited and I've thought. What happens next?"

"Nothing," the kingfisher told her. "Keep doing it. That's what you have to learn. That's what I have to teach."

"But what about the fish?" asked the little one.

The old one shrugged. "Fish are like poems, you catch them when they leap."

Frog Life

*O*nce there was a frog called Lily White who, when she contemplated her own splendour, sometimes fainted with the intensity, the immensity, the degree of it.

There were times when she wondered whether it was perhaps a little unfair that gifts which might have been apportioned more equally among frogs, had been solely lavished on her.

"Why me?" she would cry out in her solitary passion. "Why me?" And she would look about her, only to find that the other frogs were taking no notice at all. There they were, leaping and laughing and lounging about near the pond. Was it possible that they genuinely didn't mind? Or was it just that they were incapable of appreciating all they had missed?

"Can you forgive me?" she would call out to them. "Can you forgive me?"

Occasionally a passing frog would stop to reply, "Of course we forgive you. Don't worry about a thing."

Lily White would then compare herself with the nondescript frog. "B-b-but," she would begin, "I'm so bright and beautiful..."

"Of course you are," the frog would agree, and dive into the pond.

Lily White was baffled. "I must live with the sweetest natured frogs in the whole world," she would say to herself. "But no – that's impossible – their coarseness precludes it."

She decided in the end that all the frogs in the pond were blind. "True percipience," she deduced, "must be one of the gifts they lack." The more she thought about it, the more sorry she felt. "Poor things," she murmured, "surely in this respect, at least, I owe it to them to descend to their level."

After that she took to sunning herself with her own eyes shut tight. At first she was troubled that she wasn't suffering. But she stopped worrying about that once she realised that it was only because her virtue was being rewarded. She seldom spoke to the other frogs now.

Life went on peacefully. Then, one day, a stork found the pond. All the other frogs dived for safety, but Lily White, concentrating on her own worth, stayed where she was, unaware of the stork.

The stork was charmed, and, with a great flapping of wings, seized her. When the commotion was over and the stork had flown away, the frogs surfaced and went on with their ordinary lives. As for Lily White, she ascended ever upwards, held in the stork's beak, and ecstatic that her existence had at last been fulfilled. She died happy in the knowledge that no frog had ever risen so high.

Bird Woman

Once there was a child who sprouted wings. They sprang from her shoulder blades, and at first they were vestigial. But they grew rapidly, and in no time at all she had a sizeable wing span. The neighbours were horrified.

"You must have them cut," they said to her parents.

"Why?" said her parents.

"Well, it's obvious," said the neighbours.

"No," said the parents, and this seemed so final that the neighbours left.

But a few weeks later the neighbours were back.

"If you won't have them cut, at least have them clipped."

"Why?" said the parents.

"Well, at least it shows that you're doing something."

"No," said the parents, and the neighbours left.

Then for the third time the neighbours appeared.

"On at least two occasions you have sent us away," they informed the parents, "but think of that child. What are you doing to the poor little thing?"

"We are teaching her to fly," said the parents quietly.

For Christine Mary, who was hurt as a child, but who survived, and is lovely.

— *Suniti*

Blue and Other Stories
ISBN 978-93-5046-148-8
© *text* Suniti Namjoshi
© *art* Nilima Sheikh
First published in India, 2012

Acknowledgements
Kingfisher previously published in *Kavya Bharati*, Madurai, India, 2008. *Bird Woman* first published in *Feminist Fables*, 1981. *Frog Life* first published in *Sycorax*, Penguin, India, 2006. Permission to publish, where needed, is gratefully acknowledged.

All rights reserved. No part of this book may be reproduced or used in any form or by any means — graphic, electronic or mechanical — without the prior written permission of the publisher.

Published by
Tulika Publishers, 24/1 Ganapathy Colony Third Street, Teynampet, Chennai 600 018, India
email tulikabooks@vsnl.com *website* www.tulikabooks.com

Printed and bound by
Sudarsan Graphics, 27 Neelakanta Mehta Street, T. Nagar, Chennai 600 017, India

Blue and Other Stories

BY Suniti Namjoshi

ART Nilima Sheikh